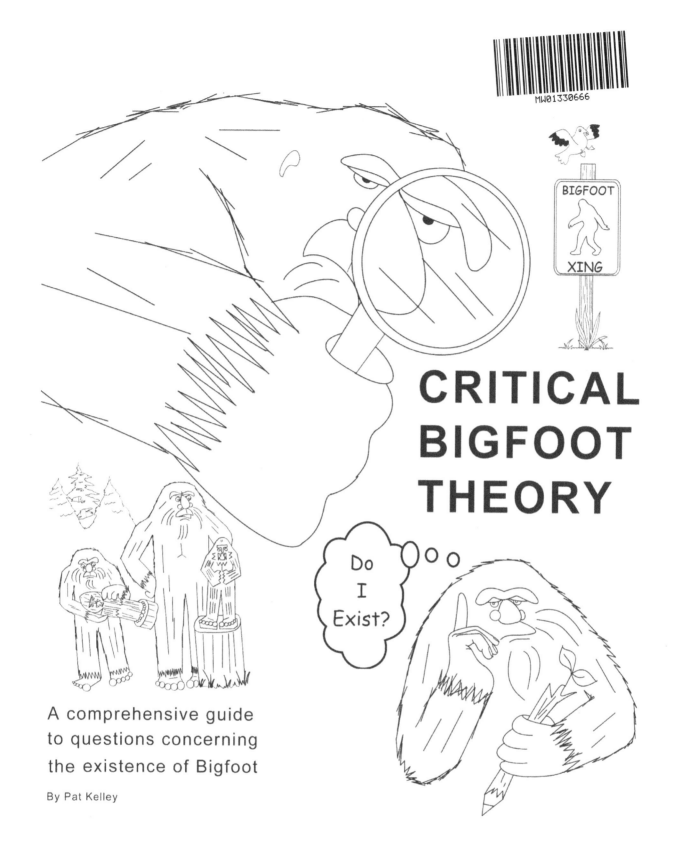

CRITICAL BIGFOOT THEORY

A comprehensive guide to questions concerning the existence of Bigfoot

By Pat Kelley

CRITICAL BIGFOOT THEORY

DOES BIGFOOT EXIST?

Bigfoot Kilroy Was Here

DEDICATION

Dedicated to my Father,
Robert Kelley,
who instilled endless curiosity
and emphasized the importance
of not taking things at face value
and, when in doubt, to always
ask questions.

Many thanks to
Adria Gaebrialla
Anne Sanders
for providing expert proofreading,
editing, comments, questions
and guidance

Table of Contents

Preface — 5
    Why Synergetic Marketing Matters — 9
    The Importance of Critical Thinking — 10
Enter, Critical Bigfoot Theory — 13
    A Brief History of the 5 W's and One H Method — 13
Bigfoot Guide to Critical Thought — 14
    Is Bigfoot an Alien Species? — 15
Introduction to Critical Bigfoot theory — 16
Critical Thought — 16
Critical Thinkers Think Objectively — 18
Make Reasoned, Rational Decisions — 19
    How to Research Bigfoot (and anything else) — 20
    Questions to Ask, Things to Watch Out For: — 22
    Begin Critical Thought with the Basics: — 22
Memories, Assumptions and Stereotypes — 24
Decision Grid: Visualize How Decisions are Made — 25
Introducing PlinkoBrain — 25
    Potential Physical & Emotional Roadblocks — 27
Things to consider before you begin — 28
Is Bigfoot real? — 28
    GRID 1: External Question: First Element, the Questions to ask — 31
    This is where the 5 W's and one H come in handy. — 32
    GRID 2: Internal: Bring to Mind — 33
    GRID 3: Virtual Contemplation — 36
    GRID 4: Fourth Element: Decision, Response: — 55
Research Resources — 61
    About the author — 64

PREFACE

THINK ABOUT THINKING

The purpose of Critical Bigfoot Theory is to provide a guideline to critical thought. Critical thinking helps individuals develop questions to ask when one is confronted by outrageous claims.

The goal of Critical Bigfoot Theory is not to convince a reader whether Bigfoot is real or not but to introduce the skills necessary to think and reason critically about whether such a creature could exist and learn to apply these questioning skills to any subject at hand.

The author currently resides in the Pacific Northwest, near Jedediah State park, California, aka Bigfoot country, where legends and myths blend seamlessly with marketing and commerce.

One doesn't travel far around here before encountering images of fierce, menacing Sasquatch and Bigfoot creatures on highway billboards, statues, artworks, coffee mugs, books, buttons and bangles, including Hello Bigfoot Colorbook, and Critical Bigfoot Theory.
 Legends of big, hairy beasts wandering the wilderness are shared not only here, but in nearly every country worldwide.

The Bigfoot legend, also known as Sasquatch, goes by many names, Snowbeast, Yeti, etc., the list is quite long.

A few commonly known names for Bigfoot creatures include:

- Stinkaboo
- Swampland's Stinkman
- Abominable Snowman
- Yowie
- Nantinaq
- Skunk Ape

Myths, stories and legends provide easy explanations for the unknown. All legends have one thing in common, they offer simplistic explanations for fear of the unknown.

Like all good myths that stick around, the legend of Bigfoot seems to satisfy a need to explain the unfamiliar event

- Distant sounds of crashing deep in the woods
- The howl of an unseen forest animal
- Campgrounds ransacked in the night

Stories and legends also provide a rich inventory of fantastic magic, mysterious and, mostly harmless, ghost and monster stories designed to suspend our disbelief.

Such stories also scare the Bejeezus out of children at the campfire, and how much fun is that, really? A real win/win in the book of successful parenting tactics.

If we were to write down all the Earthly mythologies the list would circle the Earth 1,000 times, maybe 10,000?

How many mythologies are there and where do they start?

My theory is the first myth started with the discovery of how to make and control fire.

Early humans would gather around the nightly camp fire all huddled together to keep warm and then one guy told a story that scared the Begeezus out of the kids and a tradition was born.

More probable theory is that mythologies are fantastic stories of magic and miracles, superheros and saviors mixed with real and imagined events that are shared through song, poetry, stories, movies and word-of-mouth throughout history.

Some myths and legends date back into antiquity, origins unknown.

Bigfoot legendary serves as the criteria for this critical thought exercise because in these stomping grounds, the Pacific Northwest, the character of Bigfoot is well known and loved and fun to discuss. No shortage of food for thought.

THINK ABOUT THINKING...

Bigfoot Cub Plays with a Wendigo

Mythologies are shared through song, poetry, stories, movies and word-of-mouth.

Have you heard stories about these mysterious creatures?

Fairies, Werewolves, Wendigos, Thunderbirds, Pixies, Tiny forest people, Nymphs, Troglodytes, Giant Mountain People, Leprechauns, Hairy-faced dwarfs, Space Alien UFOs (Unidentified Flying Objects), Elves, Angels, Vampires, Ghosts, Devils, Huan Do, Shape Shifters, Gremlins, Trolls, Flying Spaghetti Monster, Mermaids, Chupacabras, Loch Ness Monster, Santa Claus, Tooth Fairy, Unicorn

Do you believe any of these stories are true? Do you believe these creatures exist?

Questions to Ask:

- Why do people believe in mythological creatures?
- Do you believe in the existence of mythological creatures?
- Do you know anyone who believes in mythological creatures?
- Which legends, if any, are based upon fact?

Problems may arise when people actually believe tall tales and fanciful stories are true or based upon actual events.

Every myth contains its own collection of fanciful and mysterious entities. This is where critical thinking skills become most important. Critical thinking is the act of not simply accepting at face value what we are shown, told, what we hear or what we think.

Critical thought enables individuals to recognize tall tales, puffery, exaggerated claims. To recognize obfuscations and embellishments and realize these are designed to discourage the finer art of questioning our own better judgement.

Mix Bigfoot mythology with modern marketing, then fasten your seatbelts. Legends that once traveled on foot campfire to campfire are now hurling through space at warp speed to awaiting devices worldwide.

THINK ABOUT THINKING…
SUSPENSION OF DISBELIEF MAKES THE WORLD GO AROUND

The invention of synergistic marketing in the 1930's advanced marketing technology 100 fold. Commercial advertising has evolved into near predatory behavior which makes Critical Bigfoot Theory nearly a psychological survival guide to sanity.

Technology enables marketers to morph communication into interconnected arrays of networks designed to connect to every aspect of humanity. These networks employ tactics designed to manipulate, motivate, mold and maneuver in order to grasp attention to form permanent brand marketing bonds. Emphasis on unthinking attention.

Social media distractions

Synergetic, multi-layered advertising is now the gold standard that employs all sorts of stimuli guaranteed to touch our hot buttons in order to incite and influence to buy, sell, act, believe, vote, etc.

Simultaneous Stimuli include:

- Color, recognition of logos and brands
- Sense of smell, eg the odors from bakery
- Nostalgia, association with loving memories
- Emotions, fear, unease motivates sales
- Product placement in media to establish familiarity
- Social media, word of mouth, celebrity recommendation to establish a trust bond
- Advertising, billboards, flyers, mailers
- Rumor, false claims, innuendo designed to cast doubt
- Us against them, divisive class, ethnic, morality reminders

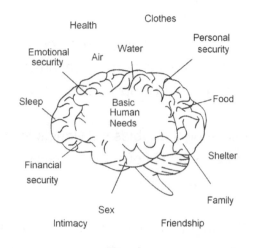

Think About Thinking…

WHY SYNERGETIC MARKETING MATTERS

Synergetic marketing techniques combine to intentionally target basic human needs at every level. These techniques are employed in order to purposely manipulate emotions, instill fear and doubt, all for the low price of, oh, only the control over the very thoughts in our heads.

In marketing, the pros provided are very strong while the cons are virtually non-existent. Usually, only the parts of the story that sell the products or prove the point are included in the sales pitch.

Marketers, politicians, advertisers, hucksters and con artists alike count and depend upon the gullibility of people who don't think about thinking. Synergetic, multi-level-marketing thrive on simplistic, either/or, fight or flight, 2-Dimensional solutions. Critical 3-D thought adds depth by introducing personal growth and self control into the equation.

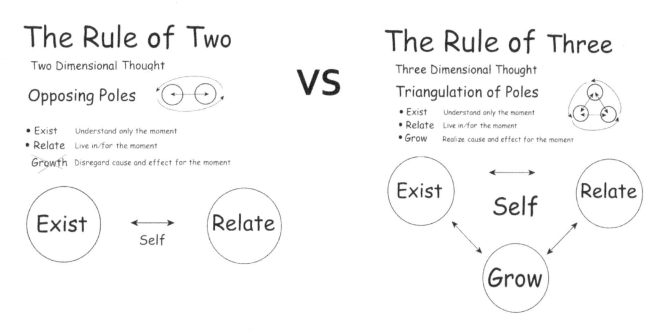

Think About Thinking…
Puffery and Fluffery

Consider the difference between the photo of your favorite hamburger and fries combo and the product you actually receive.

With advertising and marketing, photos of food and the actual product rarely match because the food in the photo is rarely real food. Marketing photos of food are artist renditions of tasty dishes filled with inedible additions, glue, varnish, paint, all for the purpose of appealing to the camera.

Few people complain or seem to notice advertising deceptions because the food is convenient, fast, quick, easy, generally tasty, plus we've been pre-conditioned to feel hunger through marketing, so we overlook the fluffery and puffery.

Legends of Bigfoot, Sasquatch, Yeti, by any other name, could be considered puffery yet harmless entertainment for the most part. Which makes this CBT project that much more enjoyable.

The Importance of Critical Thinking
What is Critical Thinking?

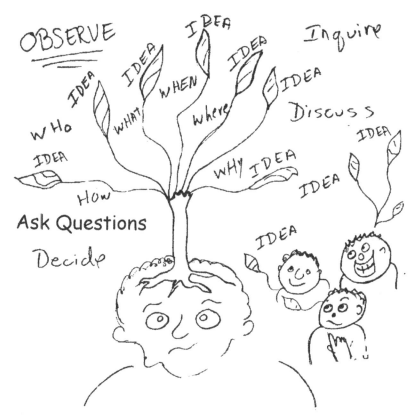

Critical thinking is the kind of thinking in which a person questions, analyzes, interprets, evaluates and makes judgement about what they read, hear, say, write and, most importantly, think.

In a nutshell, critical thinkers think about thinking and then share what they think with others.

Critical Thinking sounds kind of complicated if you don't really think critically about critical thought.

If you search the Internet for the term "critical thought," within seconds you'll receive an overwhelming 2 to 3 million descriptions and links to explanations and examples of critical thought.

Understandably, a novice to the technique of critical thinking might feel overwhelmed, intimidated by the sheer onslaught of choices with explanations ranging from crystal clear, easy to understand, to nearly unintelligible, overly complicated mental gymnastics.

KISS KEEP IT SIMPLE, SILLY

With Internet searches, the first results are mostly paid placements, not always the best or most accurate results. Learn to recognize and appreciate simplicity. Search engine optimization services often skew results for a multitude of reasons, politics and social engineering have their effects.

Search algorithms are written by humans and humans are prone to biased thinking which in turn can skew results in favor of a programmer's particular ideological bent.

The acronym KISS, the only acronym I truly appreciate, says it best. Simplicity frees the mind to concentrate on fun stuff like imagination, creativity, inquiry which may only thrive in freedom of thought. Keep KISS in mind as you peruse critical thought search results. Don't waste brain space on overly complicated explanations, just skip over in favor of clear, understandable information.

These important questions form the basics of critical analysis to better determine whether a thing is true or false. Journalists, reporters, investigators and researchers are routinely taught the 5W's and 1H.

Journalism degrees and educational papers are not necessary to learn critical thinking skills and apply to aspects of everyday life. Most people can learn to ask questions when faced with dubious claims and think critically of the responses to inquiry.

ENTER, CRITICAL BIGFOOT THEORY

The publication Critical Bigfoot Theory explores the legend of Bigfoot/Sasquatch through the lens of critical thought and provides a guideline on steps necessary to develop critical thinking skills. Exploration begins with the basics to critical thought, the 5w's and 1h rule.

- Who
- What
- When
- Where
- Why
- How

A Brief History of the 5 W's and One H Method

The concept of asking critical questions was introduced in 1560 by English rhetorician Thomas Wilson (1524-1581), who introduced the method as the "Seven Circumstances" of medieval rhetoric:

> *Who, what, and where, by what helpe, and by whose,*
> *Why, how and when, doe many things disclose.*
> — *The Arte of Rhetorique, 1560*

These Seven Circumstances were updated to the current 5W & 1H by Rudyard Kipling's famous poem:

> "I Keep Six Honest Serving Men" (*The Elephant's Child*) which was published in the April 1900 of Ladies Home Journal.

The who, what, when, where, why and how questions form the absolute basics of critical thought.

BIGFOOT GUIDE TO CRITICAL THOUGHT

The question begins: Does Bigfoot exist? We've heard the rumors and rumblings, seen the statues, read the tall tales, watched the scary movies, pondered the blurry photos for thousands of years, yet hard, actual proof remains elusive.

It is a pretty safe bet most people reach maximum belief saturation point around the ages of 8 to 10 years of age about such fanciful entities as:

- Santa Claus
- Easter Bunny
- Leprechauns
- Trolls under bridges
- Tooth Fairies
- Angels
- Vampires
- Werewolves
- Boogie men

So, what's the deal with Bigfoot?

WHAT MAKES BIGFOOT SO SPECIAL?

It's a mystery why so many people apparently believe that Bigfoot exists.
What makes Bigfoot so special to be able to survive in our imaginations?
Why does the possibility of Bigfoot strike fear in the hearts of intrepid hikers and campers who dare trek far into the vast hinterlands of the Pacific Northwest and Canada?

Is Bigfoot just a scary Boogie Man or is there really a wild, smelly, gigantic apelike creature lurking in the shadows waiting to create havoc upon campgrounds and lay waste to innocent intruders?

This book explores the possibilities with a critical eye and asks the questions necessary to help the reader reach logical, rational and reasonable conclusions.

Is Bigfoot an Alien Species?

As a skeptic of paranormal and superstitious happenings, this author's instincts say Bigfoot does not exist, and yet, I readily partake in the fantasy monster genre should a new movie or a discovery of interest cross my path.

I also enjoy stories of UFO's alien hunters and super hero characters and am a fan of Ancient Alien Astronaut theory. I'm a sucker for a good story, just like everybody else, after all, who am I to ruin a good fantasy?

All I ask is that you think a bit about the rumblings, the statues, the tall tales, the movies, and all those blurry photos and take the stories with a grain of salt...with salt being critical thinking.

Don't just take someone's word for it, ask the right questions.

- Who
- What
- When
- Where
- Why
- How

Space Alien Ship Beams Bigfoot Cubs Out to the Playground

PS: When developing a new habit, repetition is important. When in doubt, ask and keep on asking.

INTRODUCTION TO CRITICAL BIGFOOT THEORY

Who is Bigfoot? What is Bigfoot?

Bigfoot is believed to be a giant, mysterious, ill-tempered, smelly, destructive and hairy mountain beast that lives in seclusion in the forests of Northern California and the greater Pacific Northwest.

We have Questions

How can such a creature exist but never seems to be found?

Is Bigfoot real or a myth like the Tooth Fairy and forest elves?

If Bigfoot is ape-like, and ape-like creatures rely on family and community to survive, where is Bigfoot's community? What is Bigfoot's family tree?

Who teaches Bigfoot how to survive in the wilderness?

Too Many Questions

Critical Bigfoot Theory explores the possibilities of the who, what, when, where, why and how such an ape-man creature might exist.

What kind of social community or family the creature might require.

Explore the pros and cons of Bigfoot as we follow the antics and adventures of the improbability of the existence of a Bigfoot community hidden deep in the forests of the Pacific Northwest and California's Jedediah Smith Redwood park.

CRITICAL THOUGHT

To begin the journey, let's start with defining critical components of critical thought.

What is Critical Thought?

Critical thought is the ability to analyze information in order to formulate judgments, opinions and create solid arguments.

Critical Thinkers:

- Use **reason** to arrive at conclusions
- Study **criteria** to discern and separate fact from fiction
- Think about their own thought processes
- Ask questions:
- **Who, What, When, Where, Why and How**

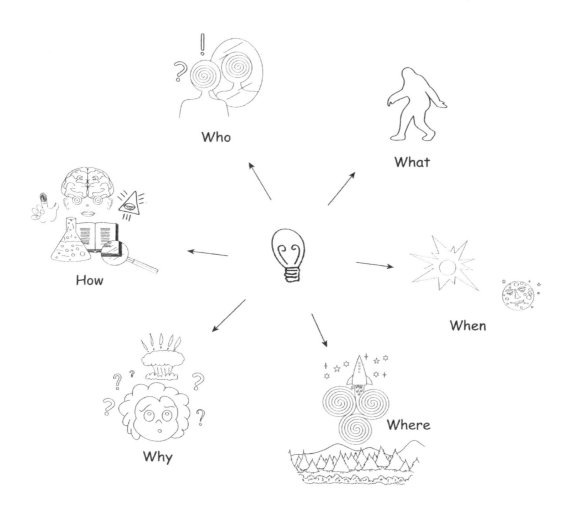

CRITICAL THINKERS THINK OBJECTIVELY

In order to reach logical conclusions we must strive to think **objectively,** not **subjectively,** in order to make decisions based upon facts or reality.

What is the definition of objective and subjective, and how do they differ?

Objective:
- Existing; actual or real, not hypothetical or imagined.
- Based on observable phenomena; empirical.
- Not influenced by emotions or personal prejudices

Subjective:
- Non-existent, hypothetical and imagined
- Opinions, conclusions based upon personal experiences or feelings

How to begin to think objectively

- Examine the evidence
- Ask the 5W's and 1H questions
- Be prepared to change your mind about things you already know
- Keep it simple (KISS)

MAKE REASONED, RATIONAL DECISIONS

WHAT ARE DECISIONS?

Definitions of the term "Decision" include:

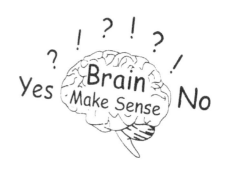

- Conclusions or judgments reached after consideration of a subject
- Passing of judgment on issues under consideration
- Action or determination

Decisions occur when we accept or are receptive to information and events that successfully challenge our established assumptions, stereotypes and or paradigms.

Example: I received new information and decided to change my mind.

In order to make good decisions, we must research what is known about the subject, in this case, Bigfoot, to ascertain what resources and tools are available and whether the sources are credible.

What are available resources for gathering information about Bigfoot?

How can we tell when a resource is credible?

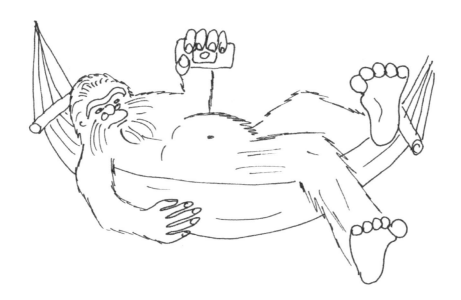

Bigfoot relaxes in a hammock to take a selfie.

Question: Is this Bigfoot in a hammock with a camera scenario credible? Believable?

How to Research Bigfoot (and anything else)

Knowing how to <u>research</u> is an extremely useful skill to learn. When you know what tools are available, you can solve problems by yourself instead of waiting or relying upon others to do the work for you.

- Find a topic - in this case Bigfoot
- Refine the topic - what do we want to know about Bigfoot
- Locate sources related to your topic, where to find sources
- Learn about the tools available to assist in research, programs, applications, card files etc., that can help organize and store your work

Bigfoot Walks in the wilderness

TYPES OF RESOURCES

The invention of the Internet has taken much of the legwork out of the art of research but keep in mind that most internet* resources are not regulated for quality or accuracy. Many more resources are hidden behind paywalls that require subscriptions and dues.

In addition to the convenience of the Internet, these resources, below, are among the most reliable, tried and true forms of information gathering, analytical tools.

Definitions of types of resources:

- Dictionary, provides an alphabetical list of words with meanings and pronunciation
- **Thesaurus**, lists words in groups of synonyms and antonyms
- **Encyclopedia**, give comprehensive information on topics of knowledge in alphabetical order
- **Trade magazines or newspapers** discuss specific topics or cover particular trades or industries
- **Professional research papers** provide analysis, interpretation, and argument based on in-depth independent research
- **Amateurs, enthusiasts.** People who do things for enjoyment, not pay
- **Eye witness reports** given by people of events they have personally witnessed
- **Historical documents** original sources about people, places or events that provide important accounts of historical methodology
- **Word of mouth**, literature passed verbally from person to person, through poems and songs, myths, dramas, rituals, proverbs, riddles, tales, fables, legends
- **Internet* web sites,** information available on the Internet, includes media, blogs, personal experiences - information given is not always accurate or responsible.
- **Books and magazines** nonfiction books, specialty magazines provide general information from broad overviews to deep analysis of a subject
- **Libraries** traditional buildings that house collections of books & media used for reading and study, also online libraries

* Internet resources are generally not reviewed for accuracy or responsibility.

QUESTIONS TO ASK, THINGS TO WATCH OUT FOR:

Bad information, disinformation, false stories spread quickly thanks to instant electronic data sharing. Such foolishness is not limited to Bigfoot lore. Any subject can become misconstrued to create the illusion of truth and fact.

Deceivers generally provide only the parts of the story that support their opinion or sell their products. Products commonly differ in appearance from their photographs due to puffery, and it is legal, mostly. Advertising puffery thrives and depends upon the trust and gullibility of people who don't think much about thinking.

These are a few examples of the many ways deceivers try to deceive, obfuscate and otherwise muddy the waters of research.

Warning Bells & Whistles:
If you see too many of these tactics, put on your tinfoil skeptic's hat and be wary:

- **Blurry and altered** or photo-shopped photographs.
- **Manipulative words** that target emotional responses and trigger cognitive biases. **Manipulative language** may indicate the writer is more interested in conversion, persuasion, indoctrination rather than education.
- **Propaganda** often takes advantage of cognitive biases to persuade, incite, encourage, intimidate and pressure.
- **Buzz Words** that promote a particular outcome and ignore viable alternative explanations.
- **One-sided** anecdotal information, appeals to authority arguments that hide or distort facts. The pros are very strong while the cons are virtually non-existent.
- **Appeals to our senses** sight, hearing, touch, smell, taste, etc. Colors, sounds, scents can affect emotions in order to influence believably.
- **Social media influences**, friend recommendations can instill illusions of trust.
- **Lack of source attribution**. Quote supposed facts but give no link or source for the statement.

BEGIN CRITICAL THOUGHT WITH THE BASICS:

5 W's & 1 H Questions to ask

- Who is Bigfoot?
- What is Bigfoot?
- When does Bigfoot appear?
- Where does Bigfoot live?
- Why do people believe in Bigfoot?
- How can Bigfoot exist?

The only limit to questions is your own imagination and your ability to move past your own internalized assumptions and stereotypes. Plinko Brain, explained on page 25, provides visual food for thought in determining personal roadblocks that affect decision-making.

Bigfoot & Cub go Kayaking and see a Chinook Salmon

MEMORIES, ASSUMPTIONS AND STEREOTYPES

What are Memories, Assumptions and Stereotypes?

Imagine if every time you took a step you had to stop to think about lifting your other foot or wonder what to do with a fork after taking a bite of food? Obviously you would want decisions like these activities to operate on **autopilot**, automatic response, who wouldn't? That's **memory**.

Assumptions are learned lessons stored in our brains as memory clusters that communicate with each other through synaptic connections. Assumptions are subconscious survival mechanisms that manage and automate everything we do and say. **Stereotypes** are over-generalized beliefs based upon common characteristics and abilities of particular groups or classes of people.

We form autopilot memories and assumptions to events and ideas so we don't have to consciously think about things we've already learned and experienced for activities that rarely change. Some assumptions evolve into **stereotypes** which can be good or bad and once learned. Autopilot thoughts rarely change unless successfully challenged in the sudden realization,the "Aha, Eureka! I have found it," moment,

Assumptions that rarely change might include:

- Sugar is sweet
- Fire is hot
- Knives are sharp

Once these important survival lessons are learned, we automatically assume not to touch anything hot, to expect sugar to be sweet and perceive knives as sharp, no thought involved.

An example of an assumption that can change might include a negative or traumatic encounter at an early age.

Example: The author was bullied by a grumpy poodle around the age 5 and consequently developed and held onto a negative opinion about poodles in general for many years. It took accidental ownership of a sweet little toy poodle to change her mind.

Adverse occurrences about anything can lead people to develop negative assumptions and stereotypes about virtually everything. Often, it takes a positive or shock encounter to trigger the mind-changing event, or paradigm shift, that forces one to think and reconsider.

DECISION GRID: VISUALIZE HOW DECISIONS ARE MADE

Did you know, the brain never stops thinking? Decisions happen in a blink of an eye. Let's slow things down to a crawl with the Decision Grid to examine what happens in the brain's decision-making process.

This **Decision Grid** demonstrates the process our minds go through from beginning to end when we need to act upon an external stimulus or have an idea.

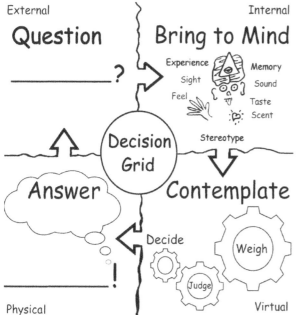

External Input: ASK
A question, emergency, subconscious reaction. Anything that requires us to provide a response.

Internal Memory: THINK
Recollection of existing experience, training, instinct, intuition, feeling.

Virtual Processing: ANALYSE
Thinking, thought. How we evaluate, compare, update existing data or incorporate new information to memory pods.

Response: DECIDE
Decision, conclusion, opinion or reaction.

Human brains have near infinite capacity for thinking, reasoning and rationality. Did you know our brains are also very creative and will sometimes make stuff up to create false memories?

Each individual's experiences are unique, therefore there are no limits to what can affect our memories and decision-making processes. Depending upon circumstance, complexity, urgency, decisions can happen in split-seconds, milliseconds or can take minutes, hours, days, weeks or years to formulate.

- Decisions Can be Influenced by:
- Personality
- Mood, Emotion, Impulse
- Degree of Complexity
- Repetition, Habit.
- Familiarity, Assumption, Stereotype
- Knowledge of Subject
- Money, Income
- Culture, Religion, Taboo

INTRODUCING PLINKOBRAIN

Roadblocks to Reason

In the Price is Right, a popular TV show, the game of Plinko demonstrates the randomness of chance.

In order to win a prize, a contestant inserts a game puck into a maze grid with bumper pads. The puck bounces off the bumper pads as it travels through the maze until ultimately falling into a category to either win a prize or place a big fat zero.

Plinko Brain Roadblocks
Conscious and Subconscious Influences

Plinko-Brain is a term that visually describes mental roadblocks that can filter our thoughts and throw barriers to restrict how clearly we think.

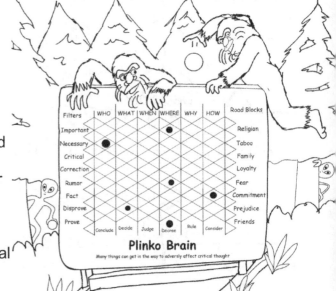

Questions, quandaries and challenges continuously float into our virtual sphere (thinking space) until the notion at hand can be either accepted and implanted as memory or rejected, neglected and forgotten, or saved for consideration. Remember the brain never stops thinking.

PlinkoBrain describes what happens when our brains receive information to consider. Our individual synaptic connections act like bumper pads that bounce thoughts through our brain's maze of memories to compare against what we already know, have experienced and saved as memorized, automatic responses.

PlinkoBrain also filters input through the senses: sound, taste, smell, sight, intuition or gut feelings to compare with our learned stereotypes.

The end results are our reactions to the information once we decide what to think, do or say.

Some simple Plinko Brain roadblock questions you might ask yourself:

- When do my roadblocks arise?
- What roadblocks convince me to believe?
- Who can I trust with my roadblocks?
- Where do my roadblocks arise?
- Why do my roadblocks arise?
- How did my roadblocks form?

POTENTIAL PHYSICAL & EMOTIONAL ROADBLOCKS

Things to think about while researching topics or processing new information:

Roadblocks to inquiry could include, but are not limited to:

Who might block or restrict access to inquiry?
> Interference or deterrence from family, friends, employers, teachers, clergy, authority, your own fear

What situations might block or restrict access to inquiry?
> Fees, dues, lack of funds, authority, physical and virtual paywalls, distance, physical effort, religious doctrine, government laws and regulations, tradition, age restrictions

When could inquiry be blocked or restricted?
> Time restrictions, physical location, hardship

Where might inquiry be blocked or restricted?
> Military bases, exclusive clubs, personality cliques, dangerous situations, licensing, degrees, fences, forbidden zones, religious doctrine, government laws or regulations

Why could inquiry become blocked or restricted?
> Safety, security, need to know, secrecy, trespass laws, dangerous situations

How could inquiry be blocked or restricted?
> Physical and virtual barriers, Authorization, license, above pay grade

Bigfoot Pranksters Make a Bigfootprint on the beach

THINGS TO CONSIDER BEFORE YOU BEGIN

Q: Is the pursuit of Bigfoot worth my time?

Q: What do I hope to accomplish?

Q: Is the study of Bigfoot interesting, relevant, necessary or beneficial and to whom?

Q: Are legends of Bigfoot creatures believable, real, plausible, fable, myth or cautionary tales?

Q: What resources are available for serious study?

Q: Are the resources available for inquiry about Bigfoot trustworthy and how do we determine validity?

Q: What are roadblocks to inquiry about Bigfoot?

Bigfoot climbs a tree

Is Bigfoot real?

The Critical Bigfoot Theory Decision Grid helps guide questions to exploration of theories logically, through step by step visualization of the thought process.

Each step in the BCT Decision Grid identifies elements specifically important to each stage of the decision-making process.

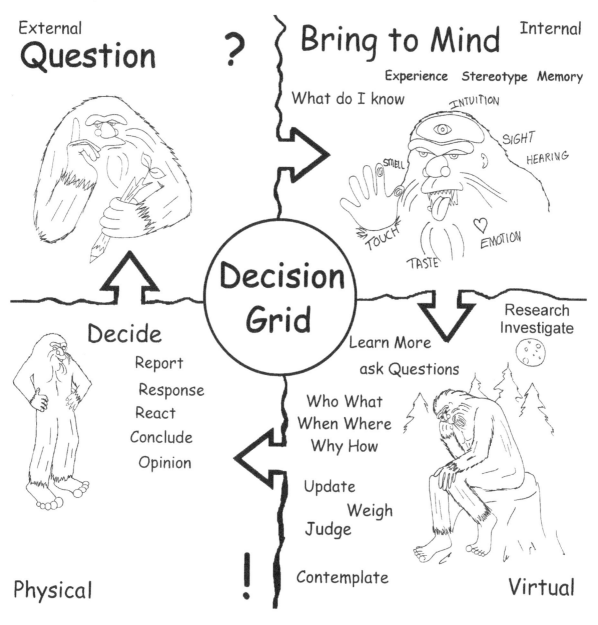

1. **External Question:**
   Ask the question:
   Does Bigfoot exist?

2. **Internal Bring to Mind:**
   Recall what you already know about Bigfoot.

3. **Virtual Contemplate:**
   Research, evaluate, compare new vs old information.

4. **Physical Response:**
   Make a decision, conclusion, opinion or reaction.

GRID 1: EXTERNAL QUESTION: FIRST ELEMENT, THE QUESTIONS TO ASK

DOES BIGFOOT EXIST?

Bigfoot asks "Do I exist?"

GRID 1: BIGFOOT CRITICAL THEORY - QUESTIONS TO ASK...

How do we know what information should be believed and which information should be questioned?

This is where the **5 W's and one H** come in handy.

How can Bigfoot exist?

- Where does Bigfoot live?
- What is real about Bigfoot?
- Why does Bigfoot hide?
- What is Bigfoot's lifespan?
- How do I find Bigfoot?

Who are Bigfoot experts?

- What qualifies a person to be a Bigfoot expert?
- What should I know about Bigfoot?
- Why do people believe in Bigfoot?
- What are hoaxes about Bigfoot
- Where is the proof, evidence and research?

What Benefits to finding Bigfoot

- Are there any benefits?
- For the experience?
- For the fun of it?
- Out of curiosity?
- For the sake of exploration?
- Excuse to commune with nature?

What questions should I ask?

- Am I afraid to find Bigfoot?
- What is there to fear?
- Is fear of Bigfoot reasonable?
    - Rational?
    - Realistic?

GRID 2: INTERNAL: BRING TO MIND
SECOND ELEMENT, THOUGHTS, MEMORY

Bigfoot experiences the states of intuition: sight, smell, hearing, touch, taste, emotion

Suggestions for Introspective Questions to Trigger Recollections:

Entertain your thoughts. Imagination the possibilities:

- What do I already know about Bigfoot?
- Who do I think Bigfoot is?
- Do I think Bigfoot is real or imaginary?
- What stereotypes have I formed based upon my assumptions of Bigfoot?
- What are my experiences with Bigfoot that I have learned or remembered through stories, movies, radio, Internet, friends, family, school, job, school?
- What do I **think** about the existence of Bigfoot?
- What does my gut, my intuitive sense tell me about Bigfoot?
- How do I **feel** about the existence of Bigfoot?

GRID 2: BRING TO MIND: Thoughts, Memories…

Should I fear Bigfoot? Why? What do I already know?

Bigfoot teaches cubs how to shake a treehouse.

GRID 2: BRING TO MIND: Thoughts, Memories…

Would I pitch a tent in isolated Bigfoot territory? Why? Why not?
Where is the best location to search for Bigfoot?
What would I bring with me in a search for Bigfoot?
- Supplies,
- weapons,
- Bug repellent,
- Camping gear,
- A friend?

Bigfoot teaches a cub how to frighten tent campers.

GRID 2: BRING TO MIND: Thoughts, Memories…

What would I do if I actually met Bigfoot? Would I be scared? Why?
What if Bigfoot turns out to be friendly?
Would I introduce myself, take a selfie or make a video?
Would I try to capture Bigfoot?

Bigfoot acts like King Kong to frighten a boater

GRID 3: VIRTUAL CONTEMPLATION
THIRD ELEMENT, PROCESSING, THINKING

Mental Consideration, how can this be possible?
- Are beliefs about Bigfoot true, based on fact, evidence?
- Are beliefs about Bigfoot based upon tenuous or anecdotal evidence?

Bigfoot Thinker

GRID 3: CONTEMPLATION, PROCESSING, THINKING…

How do accounts of Bigfoot attributes or characteristics compare between:

- Experts,
- Amateurs,
- Eye witnesses,
- Folk stories and fables?

How are these reports similar?
How are they different?

If I ever met Bigfoot, what's the worst thing that could happen?
What do I want to happen? What is the best case scenario?

How would I react to meeting Bigfoot in person?
- Would I be scared to death?
- Would I scream?
- Would I fight?
- Would I run away and hide?

What would humans do if Bigfoot is ever found?
Should Bigfoot be afraid of people?

Bigfoot and cub see an alien spaceship.

GRID 3: CONTEMPLATION, PROCESSING, THINKING…

What's the Worst That Can Happen in the Search for Bigfoot?

What is there to fear in the wilderness besides Bigfoot?
Life in the wilderness is fun but can be dangerous because if a person gets injured, emergency services can be hours or days away.

What kinds of dangers can happen in areas isolated away from modern civilization?

Bigfoot Says "Hello"

GRID 3: CONTEMPLATION, PROCESSING, THINKING…

Danger can be both real and imagined.

REAL, RATIONAL DANGERS - NATURE IN THE RAW

Weather: snow, ice, rainstorms, hail, avalanches, floods, lightning, forest fires.

Animals: *predatory*, meat-eating carnivorous wolves, coyotes, bears, big cats, snakes, badgers. Animals that might think of people as a handy snack.

Animals: *herbivores*, such as moose, deer, bison with horns and hooves. Animals that might resent intrusion upon their territories.

Humans: reclusive forest dwelling people who might resent intrusion, traffic from logging trucks and recreational vehicles where operators don't expect to be intruded upon.

Insects: blood-sucking, disease-carrying, stinging and biting mosquitoes, scorpions, ticks, spiders. Insects that might appreciate intrusion of warm-blooded intruders for their supper.

A hungry wolf in the wilderness can be very dangerous

GRID 3: CONTEMPLATION, PROCESSING, THINKING...
IMAGINARY, IRRATIONAL DANGERS

Unidentified Noises in the Night: Sudden, unusual sounds in the night can strike fear into the strongest heart. Unknown noises are disturbing enough but add superstition and fear to the mix of an active imagination and campfire stories of legend are born. Where legendary dangers slip into the **irrational zone where** the slightest noises magnify and shadows become ominous, threatening creatures.

<u>Sensory deprivation</u>. When one or more of our senses; taste, touch, smell, hearing, and sight, becomes reduced or completely eliminated, our minds go into overdrive to force the experience to make sense. What makes sense, however, can be a bit senseless, logically. Sensory deprivation in cave exploration, for instance, has caused some people to have hallucinations and see or hear things that do not exist.

Creatures of myths and legends possibly formed through imaginary dangers include:
Fairies, werewolves, wendigos, thunderbirds, pixies, tiny forest people, nymphs, troglodytes, giant mountain people, mythological little people, legendary pranksters hairy-faced dwarfs who supposedly live in the woods, space aliens, UFO (Unidentified Flying Objects), elves, angels, pixies, vampires, ghosts, devils, Jinn, Thunderbirds, shape shifters, gremlins, trolls, Flying Spaghetti Monster, mermaids, Chupacabras, Loch Ness monster and many, many more.

Why do people believe in mythological creatures? Is humanity seeking easy answers to mysterious questions?

Alien mermaid touches the Flying Spaghetti Monster's noodly appendage.

GRID 3: Contemplation, Processing, Thinking...

What **physical** tools are helpful to look for Bigfoot?
Always research the areas and plan ahead for the trip.
Consider this survival list as a good start.

- Field cameras are used by hunters and people who track and observe wildlife
- Security cameras are used for surveillance and security
- Dogs detect odors with their superior sense of smell
- Drones fly over areas and terrain that is virtually inaccessible to humans
- Satellite link ups
- Flashlights
- Flares
- Infrared night vision binoculars
- Sound detectors
- Movement detectors
- All terrain vehicles
- Pick axes, shovels, chain saws for clearing land or foliage
- First Aid kit
- Knives and multi-purpose tools
- Tent, tarps and twine
- Maps & Compass
- Fire starters
- Water purification tablets
- Learn which plants and fungi are safe to eat
- Learn how to catch your own food - hunting, fishing, gathering

Half of these suggestions are about personal safety and survival because, after all, a search for the elusive Bigfoot will take you deep into the wilderness and away from emergency services.

GRID 3: CONTEMPLATION, PROCESSING, THINKING…

When does Bigfoot usually appear?
What survival skills and needs happen instinctively and which must be taught?

Bigfoot and cubs catch a large Chinook Salmon

GRID 3: CONTEMPLATION, PROCESSING, THINKING…

What **physical evidence** should I look for when tracking Bigfoot?

Physical evidence might include:

- Foot prints
- Claw marks
- Hair or Fur
- Bloodstains
- Bones
- Saliva, bite marks
- Poop, scat
- Broken tree/branches,
- Disturbed vegetation
- Hidden cave, thicket or hollow log lair
- Sounds of howls and calls
- Paths and trails

Where might such evidence appear?

Baby Bigfoot bangs a drum

GRID 3: CONTEMPLATION, PROCESSING, THINKING…

What does Bigfoot do for fun?

Bigfoot rides the ocean waves on a surfboard off the coast of California

GRID 3: Contemplation, Processing, Thinking...

Where is Bigfoot's extended family or community?

Bigfoot Family Tree

GRID 3: CONTEMPLATION, PROCESSING, THINKING…
DOES BIGFOOT HAVE A COMMUNITY?

Are Bigfoot communities structured with tribal behaviors or social hierarchies with members who act as:

- Disciplinarians who punish bad behavior and reward good?
- Nurturers that provide warmth, protection, food, safety?
- Teachers of survival skills, cooperation skills, hunting, gathering, gardening?

Where are the female Bigfoot creatures and statues? Are the females smaller or larger than the males? Why don't we ever hear about female Sasquatch creatures?

Bigfoot parents play and dance with their cub

GRID 3: CONTEMPLATION, PROCESSING, THINKING…

Does Bigfoot laugh, have a sense of humor or play tricks?

Bigfoot visits the Old Shoe House with so many cubs he doesn't know what to do.

Does Bigfoot play sports?
- Climb trees?
- Jump in the water?
- Swim?

Does Bigfoot have any pets?
- Hobbies?
- Interests?
- Bird watching?
- Human watching?

GRID 3: CONTEMPLATION, PROCESSING, THINKING...

What is Bigfoot's personality?

- What was Bigfoot like as a baby, teen, juvenile, adult, old?
- Does Bigfoot feel guilt, shame, regret, sadness, joy, disappointment?
- Does Bigfoot enjoy scaring people? Why would it?
- Does Bigfoot have a religion, god, code, dance, hold rituals, mourn loss, grieve loss?
- Does Bigfoot have emotions? Sniff flowers, offer gifts, show affection, feel love, pride, jealousy, envy?

Bigfoot plays with a Monarch Butterfly

What is Bigfoot's temperament?
The rumors vary greatly. Reports of Bigfoot include a range of conflicting emotions and activities from a sweet, gentle forest guardian to a monster destroyer. Why such a variety?

- Destructive, Mysterious, ill-tempered,
- Kind and protective to forest animals
- Illusive lives in seclusion.
- Emotional range, likes, dislikes

GRID 3: Contemplation, Processing, Thinking…

Why is there such a disparity between good Bigfoot and bad Bigfoot?

What life habits does Bigfoot enjoy?

- What are Bigfoot sleep patterns?
- Does Bigfoot hibernate like bears?
- What language does Bigfoot speak?
- What sounds does Bigfoot make, sing, whistle, howl, high pitched cry,
- Can Bigfoot see in the dark?
- What food does Bigfoot eat? Fish, Nuts, Berries, Meat, Fruits?
- What are Bigfoot's favorite human foods?

Bigfoot family roast marshmallows over a campfire

GRID 3: CONTEMPLATION, PROCESSING, THINKING…

ATTRIBUTES INTELLIGENCE

How intelligent is Bigfoot? Is its intelligence equivalent to great apes? Humans? Dogs?

- Is the ability to hide from humans a sign of intelligence?
- Can Bigfoot make and extinguish or control fire?
- Does Bigfoot make tools or weapons like axes, spears, arrows, pointy sticks?
- Does Bigfoot make marks to communicate with other Bigfoot creatures, claw marks, graffiti, finger paint?
- Does Bigfoot use walking sticks, use backpacks and create tools?
- What does Bigfoot think about chainsaw art statues of Bigfoot?
- Does Bigfoot have a secret lair with TV, radio, internet, cell phone, bed?

Bigfoot and cubs examine chainsaw art statues of Bigfoot

GRID 3: CONTEMPLATION, PROCESSING, THINKING…

Attributes: What about Bigfoot's Personal Appearance & Grooming

Descriptions of Bigfoot's appearance vary depending upon who reports the sightings.

The general consensus seems to agree overall that Bigfoot:

- Has a smallish head for body size
- Is quite hairy with a wooly fur coat
- Coloring ranges from gray, brown, black, white, gray, dark to reddish brown
- Is odoriferous smelly, stinky
- Has feet up to 25 inches long and up to 8 inches wide
- Can run 35 mph
- Weighs up to 600 lbs
- Stands 6' to 15' tall
- Long hair covers the body, head and the ears
- Short hair on the face, 3" to 2' in length

Bigfoot family walks on a Bigfoot crosswalk

GRID 3: CONTEMPLATION, PROCESSING, THINKING...

Does Bigfoot have holidays or celebrations like Halloween or Thanksgiving?

Bigfoot cub cavorts with kittens on Halloween night

Does Bigfoot groom its fur?

Does Bigfoot clean its teeth after eating?

GRID 3: CONTEMPLATION, PROCESSING, THINKING...

Attributes

Where does Bigfoot live?

Habitat: Mountains, snow, forests, uninhabited, country, isolated forests of the Pacific Northwest and California's Jedediah Smith Redwood park.

- How can such a large, noisy creature exist but never be found?
- What type of shelter does Bigfoot call home?
- Possible habitats might include: Caves, shallow rocky caverns, hollow trees, hollow logs, burrows, dugouts, thickets, underwater like a beaver, tree house, abandoned cabins, tents.
- Mysterious habitats might include spirit sounds, spaceships, and other dimensions.

Bigfoot and family enjoy a visit to a drive-through tree in the redwood forest.

GRID 4: FOURTH ELEMENT: DECISION, RESPONSE:
WHAT WE MIGHT CONCLUDE AFTER A THOROUGH INVESTIGATION.

Item: No Bigfoot community has ever been discovered. No conclusive proof of life or evidence of house, burrow, cave, den, shelters under bridges have ever been found.

    Possible Conclusion: Bigfoot might be an expert architect. Is this plausible?

Item: Sightings by witnesses have not been confirmed by experts.

    Possible Conclusion: Bigfoot is an expert at camouflage. Is this possible?

Item: No conclusive evidence of bones, blood, sewage, damage, carnage trails, footprints or physical evidence.

Item: Bigfoot has never captured

    Possible Conclusion: Bigfoot might be an expert planner. Is this conceivable?

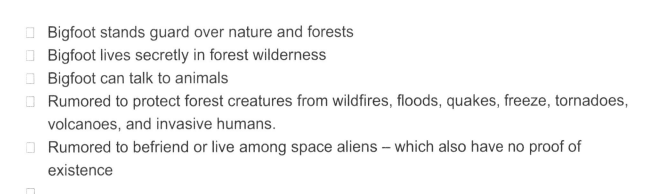

Item: Unvalidated rumors and theories about Bigfoot that can't be empirically tested:

- ☐ Bigfoot stands guard over nature and forests
- ☐ Bigfoot lives secretly in forest wilderness
- ☐ Bigfoot can talk to animals
- ☐ Rumored to protect forest creatures from wildfires, floods, quakes, freeze, tornadoes, volcanoes, and invasive humans.
- ☐ Rumored to befriend or live among space aliens – which also have no proof of existence
- ☐

Possible Conclusion: Bigfoot is expert at selective communication. Is this believable?

GRID 4: Decision, Response:

Item: Some claim that Bigfoot is a visitor from outer space. Is this out of the question? How can this make sense when alien beings have also yet to be found?

Bigfoot plays soccer with alien astronauts and a pterodactyl.

GRID 4: Decision, Response:

Item: Legend says Bigfoot is Nature's Guardian: Some say Bigfoot stands guard over nature and forests and talks to animals.

Conclusion: Bigfoot is the ultimate critical thinker who has fooled us all.

What do you think? Does this make sense?

Could it be more likely the **Probable Conclusion** is that Bigfoot does not exist and is a figment of imagination?

Bigfoot returns a baby squirrel to its nest

GRID 4: Decision, Response:

Item: Where is the <u>evidence</u> of Bigfoot?

Bigfoot uses a ruler to measure its big, giant foot

Is the fictional character, Chewbacca, the Star Wars Wookie, based upon a Bigfoot creature?

GRID 4: DECISION, RESPONSE:

More Questions:

- Things to Consider
- Things to Learn
- Good to Know

If Bigfoot is a real, flesh and blood creature, is it:

- A great ape?
- Humanoid?
- An alien?
- An ape man?

What are Bigfoot's survival needs? Does it need shelter, food, water similar to apes or humans?

What are common behaviors traits of great apes:

- Gorillas,
- Orangutans,
- Chimpanzees

How do these animal behaviors compare with Bigfoot behavior?

If Bigfoot is a great ape, and ape-like creatures rely on family and community to survive, where is Bigfoot's community?

Who teaches Bigfoot how to survive?

What foods does Bigfoot eat and drink to survive?
What are Bigfoot's natural foods?

- Vegetarian? Nuts, Berries, Fruits?
- Carnivore? Fish, Meat?
- Omnivore? All of the above?

59

GRID 4: DECISION, RESPONSE:

More things to ponder:

- Are humans, hunters and trappers more dangerous to Bigfoot than Bigfoot is to humans?

- What would humans do if Bigfoot were ever found?

- Who poses the bigger threat? Humanity or Bigfoot?

Bigfoot plays with friendly raccoons

RESEARCH RESOURCES

The Internet provides many resources for information about Bigfoot. These are just a few websites where the author found valuable contributions to topics discussed in Critical Bigfoot Theory. Disclaimer: These websites are not associated with the author, or this publication and simply included for informational purposes, with no responsibility taken for any of their content or accuracy.

- Critical Thinking https://iqexam.co/blog/critical-thinking/
- What is Propaganda? https://philosophyterms.com/propaganda/
- Why people-believe-in-bigfoot https://theconversation.com/lots-of-people-believe-in-bigfoot-and-other-pseudoscience-claims-this-course-examines-why-196919
- Color Psychology https://www.colorpsychology.org/blog/color-psychology-marketing/
- Bigfoot Propaganda https://www.sapiens.org/biology/bigfoot-hoax-public-science/
- Skeptical Inquirer - Bigfoot articles
- Recognizing Propaganda https://people.howstuffworks.com/propaganda.htm
- Great Ape Social Systems https://boisestate.pressbooks.pub/evolutionhumanbehavior/chapter/4-4-great-ape-social-systems/
- Common Bigfoot Names https://www.pararational.com/other-names-for-bigfoot/
- Little People https://en.wikipedia.org/wiki/Little_people_(mythology)
- Sasquatch https://www.britannica.com/topic/Sasquatch
- Bigfoot Body Characteristics https://bigfoot.fandom.com/wiki/Bigfoot_characteristics
- Mythical and Imaginary Creatures https://mythicalencyclopedia.com/mythical-creatures-list-a-z/
- Junior Skeptic: Bigfoot Issue https://www.skeptic.com/junior_skeptic/issue2/
- Sensory Deprivation: https://scienceofmind.org/what-happens-when-your-brain-is-deprived-of-stimulation/
- Eureka! https://www.etymonline.com/word/eureka
- Satellite https://www.starlink.com/
- Wilderness survival tools https://prepper.com/how-to-survive-in-the-wilderness-the-22-basics-of-wilderness-survival/
- Where is the evidence? https://science.howstuffworks.com/science-vs-myth/strange-creatures/bigfoot.htm

Research Resources

Links mentioned on the web version of this publication:

Emily Dickenson https://poets.org/poem/im-nobody-who-are-you-260
Adria Gaebrialla https://authoradriagaebrialla.com
Devil's Advocate https://dictionary.cambridge.org/dictionary/english/devil-s-advocate
Seven Circumstances https://www.thoughtco.com/journalists-questions-5-ws-and-h-1691205
The Elephant's Child https://www.kiplingsociety.co.uk/readers-guide/rg_elephantschild1.htm
Absolute Basics https://www.kiplingsociety.co.uk/poem/poems_serving.htm
How to Research https://collegeinfogeek.com/how-to-do-research/
Online Dictionary: https://dictionary.cambridge.org/dictionary/english/
Hello Bigfoot Colorbook https://karmacarriers.com/color-books/
Critical Bigfoot Theory https://karmacarriers.com/critical-bigfoot-theory/

Bigfoot cubs play PlinkoBrain

Bigfoot Critical Theory
Copyright © 2024 by Pat Kelley
ISBN: 9798342277990

All rights reserved. No part of this book may be reproduced or transmitted in any form or by any means without written permission from the author.

Bigfoot cub rides a hobby horse and waves goodbye.

ABOUT THE AUTHOR

I'm an ordinary, opinionated human being with a vivid imagination and penchant for investigation with a gift of gab who dabbles in the arts. For as far back as I can remember, I've always seemed to bristle at inconsistencies and hypocrisy, particularly when claims don't seem to pass the 'smell' test.

My greatest inspiration and saving grace as a lonely, somewhat isolated, socially awkward child was the Emily Dickinson poem entitled: "I'm nobody, who are you?"

This empowering poem continues to justify the energy I need to expound upon what interests me.
I have a penchant for asking questions, though not scholarly schooled in the distinguished art of critical thought, I've been blessed with a natural curiosity with a penchant for asking "why?"

Which brings me to the subject of critical thinking, a technique of thinking and reasoning taught to me early on by my Father with his Devil's Advocate style of reasoning which sparked my healthy, life-long habit of skepticism and inquiry.

Both parents made a habit of ensuring my siblings and I frequented libraries and book mobiles regularly. They also provided mountains of encyclopedias and reference books, magazines, creative arts and crafts and accompanying supplies at the ready, for our hungry brains to consume.

My main complaint at the time was their go-to response to my numerous questions invariably produced the annoying, "Go, look it up," response.

Of course, I would have appreciated everything explained to me so I wouldn't have to take the time and trouble to learn, who wouldn't, but alas, if I wanted answers I simply had to learn to "go, look it up." Thankfully, my parents provided an over abundance of access to literature.

Later, as a parent myself, I continued the annoying tradition and was heartened a few years ago when my adult child confessed he had felt similar frustration at my annoying responses to "go, look it up," at his numerous questions, but he was super appreciative of the skill as an adult.

This is where I am coming from in this publication of Critical Bigfoot Theory. My education includes study in journalism, advertising, art, plus years of experience as a Storekeeper in charge of evaluation and purchase of supplies and maintaining inventory.

My experience as an Information Systems Analyst and software tester, plus 25 years as a web designer and illustrator provides me the expertise to logically analyse problems and produce workable solutions. My interest in free thinking in the skill of skepticism is primarily self-taught.

My penchant for asking questions and sharing what I learn, the act of exposing errors and pointing out misconstrued information seems to annoy many people, but there we are. I gotta know who, what, where, why, when and how things tick or I just can't sleep at night.

The book is not so much about Bigfoot as it is about the value of critical thought and to encourage others to "go, look it up," so you can think for yourself.

Bigfoot plays a practical joke on trackers

Made in the USA
Middletown, DE
10 February 2025

71025439R00038